Going to God
Together

Going to God Together

Brendan Leahy

New City Press
of the Focolare
Hyde Park, New York

Published in the United States by New City Press
202 Comforter Blvd., Hyde Park, NY 12538
www.newcitypress.com
©2013 Brendan Leahy

Cover design by Leandro de Leon

Library of Congress Cataloging-in-Publication Data:

Leahy, Brendan, 1960-
  Going to God together / Brendan Leahy.
      pages cm
  Summary: 'Brendan Leahy offers reflections which stress undertaking the Christian
journey together and the mutual sharing of insights when we try to put the words of
the Gospel into daily practice. Leahy leads the reader to re-discover the importance
of building up the presence of Jesus among "two or more" who are going to God
together'— Provided by publisher.
  ISBN 978-1-56548-483-2 (alk. paper)
  1. Fellowship—Religious aspects—Catholic Church. 2. Christian life--Catholic
Church. I. Title.
  BV4517.5.L425 2013
  248.4'82--dc23
                                    2013016067

ISBN: 978-1-56548-483-2

Printed in the United States of America

Contents

Introduction

It's always striking to see how throughout the world, we find traces of an insatiable thirst to bow down spiritually before the Mystery that surrounds life. We see it in a Buddhist temple and in a mosque; in a Passover celebration and a Hindu *Diwali* festival. A mysterious sense of the Absolute, the transcendent, urges us to reach out beyond all that is around us, dig deep within us and, most importantly, make some form of declaration with the whole of our being that we want to be in harmony with God, with others, within ourselves.

Christians believe the Mystery has not remained nameless, but has opened up to us in the history of Israel and, above all, in the person of Jesus Christ. In him, God has been "humanized." In Jesus of Nazareth, as Benedict XVI often reminded us, we see the face of God. And Pope Francis invites us to go out and show that merciful and compassionate face to many.

Throughout the past two millennia, followers of Jesus have put his words and teachings into practice, celebrated the memory of his death and resurrection and looked forward to his coming again. The Holy Spirit has brought about many spiritual movements that have enriched Christians with ways of shaping their day-to-day relationship with God and with others in a manner that gives meaning and harmony to their own lives.

One such work of the Spirit offering a "new way" is the Focolare Movement with its communitarian spirituality.[1] It stresses going to God together and sharing with one another experiences of the Gospel lived. This spirituality, which came to life around Chiara Lubich (1920-2008) and her companions, is now lived by many around the world.[2] I too am grateful for having met this spirituality, which has helped me greatly in life.

We go to God together. In offering the reflections that follow, I am very much indebted to those with whom I have journeyed and continue to journey in the light of Jesus' promise: "Where two or more are gathered in my name, there am I among them" (Mt 18:20). They are simple reflections mirroring various moments of discovery along the Way (discoveries I need constantly to renew). Also included among the meditations are extracts from various saints and spiritual writers, both past and present, who have influenced me.

I hope that those who read these reflections may be encouraged in some small way. Jesus made a promise that wherever "two or more" are united, he is there. He who is the Way wants to be the Wayfarer among us. He wants to let us allow him to travel with us and among us. Living together the art of loving that his Gospel brings, opens the door for him to enter into our lives and dwell among us.

1

Putting God
in the First Place

The Human Journey

Humanity continues on a journey that is both beautiful and disastrous. But, as I believe that the universe and humanity have been well made, that they contain within them elements of balance and healing, there is undoubtedly another way which is unfolding and which will help each one of us, all of us together, to find a new equilibrium and inner peace. This new way which is unfolding will certainly lead human beings to the discovery of a communion that is deeper than fleeting experiences; a communion that involves permanence, covenant, fidelity; a communion that is creativity, liberty, light and life; a communion that is celebration. And this new way will lead to the discovery of a God not "up there" in the heavens, whom we can only reach through self-denial and obedience to laws, but of a God of love hidden like a tiny child at the heart of creation, at the heart of human suffering, at the heart of daily life.

Jean Vanier[3]

What Do You Desire?

The conversation between Francis and Clare of
    Assisi that always strikes me:
"What is it you desire?" asked Francis.
"God"
 replied the young Clare of Assisi.
And this brief exchange
launched Clare into a new life.
The beautiful eighteen year old,
full of hopes and dreams
knew how to envelop the desires of her heart
in the one Being truly worthy of our love:
God who is Love.

When I place myself eavesdropping on that
    conversation,
I hear an invitation:
"Love me with *all* your heart and mind and
    strength."

But then comes a question: is there a specific way
today that pleases God, a summary commandment for the modern, quick-moving world?
I recall a married couple sharing how they try
in specific, small everyday ways to live out their
love for one another throughout the whole day.
In doing so, they discover the invisible but real
presence of Jesus among them.

So I remember John's Gospel and the summary
    commandment Jesus offers:

"If you really want to love me, love one another. This is *my* commandment and it's always *new*." I too am called to envelop the desires of my heart in God, a love expressed then in love for one another.

The Crib's Invitation

The simplicity of the Christmas scene catches
  me off guard.
Coming to the crib,
I gaze and try to take in the mystery of what I see.
But there's the paradox.
It's I who has to let myself be taken into what I
  do not see.
"Do not try to enclose me within yourself but try
  to enclose yourself within me."
I remember these words that, towards the end of
her life, Teresa of Avila felt God had addressed
to her.
God is who I long for.
But God is not to be domesticated
to fit my expectations or inspections.
God is other.
God is ever more.
God is not simply what I see.
God is not the sun, the stars, the moon ...
God is indeed beyond all.
And yet, and yet ... God *is* to be found
in the universal form of his Incarnate Son
hidden and really present in each neighbor.
Yes, God is not far away beyond the clouds.
God is near.
In ways I often don't expect.
Pope Leo the Great expressed this many centu-
  ries ago:
"The Son of God ... stooped down to take up our
  lowliness ...

He remained what he was; he took up what he
was not ...
Lowliness is taken up by greatness, weakness by
power, mortality by eternity."[4]

Yes, with its divine-human invitation, the paradox of the crib appeals:
"Enclose yourself within me, not me within you ...
and I am in each neighbor."

Fighting with Perseverance

William Booth, the founder of the Salvation Army, stirs a deep chord of the soul when we hear him cry out:

> While women weep, as they do now, I'll fight;
>
> while children go hungry, as they do now, I'll fight;
>
> while men go to prison, in and out, in and out, as they do now, I'll fight;
>
> while there is a drunkard left, while there is a poor lost girl upon the streets, while there remains one dark soul without the light of God, I'll fight,
>
> I'll fight to the very end![5]

It's a stirring conviction. There is a justified indignation at seeing situations of deprivation, injustice and suffering. I too want to overcome evil with good. Faith makes me want, as the letter to Timothy puts it, "to fight the good fight" (1 Tim 6:12).

And to fight to the end, I need perseverance in faith, the perseverance that gains life.

Entering into God

Bonaventure, the great Franciscan saint, offers a true key to life when he writes: "No one enters rightly into God except through the Crucified Christ."[6]

Yes, the Crucifix reminds us of that.

It is not merely a wooden ornament; it points to a person: The Crucified Christ.

There are all kinds of ways I can try to enter into God,

but in truth they can be distractions ...

So each day I am given the chance to choose the right way,

the way of crossing over (the Crucifix) from focus on self to the neighbor,

from wanting only my own way to the will of God for me.

To cast a glance at the Crucified One,

and follow him

is to be in God.

And so to discover myself fully in God's cruciform logic of love.

Three Supports for True Love

At a certain age,
when the human heart and body are beating new
    in emotion and impulse,
I needed to hear about the *purity* of love and
    relationship.
When I have found myself beginning to cling to
    possessions of all types
it has been necessary to hear about *poverty,*
and then later still
when tasks, projects and ideas
have begun to take over
it has been vital to hear about *obedience*
(perhaps the most difficult word!).
Yes, life has its stages
spiralling ever new through life's journey.
God is not other persons, nor things, nor oneself.
God wants me to be a gift to others just as he has
    created my neighbor as a gift for me.
Purity, poverty, obedience —
three supports for a life of giving and receiving
    in faith, hope and love,
true love of God and of neighbor.
To build on these three supports requires
conversion of what Yeats calls the "rag and bone
    shop of the heart"
where "all the ladders start."
Conversion...
by rekindling
belief in the primacy of the "first love,"
the Love,

the one-not-to-be-divided Love:
God-Love.

It is I who answer and look after you ... Your
faithfulness comes from me (Hos 14:8).

2

Cast Everything
onto the Father

Father, I Abandon Myself into Your Hands

Father,
I abandon myself into your hands;
do with me what you will.
Whatever you may do, I thank you:
I am ready for all, I accept all.
Let only your will be done in me,
and in all your creatures —
I wish no more than this, O Lord.

Into your hands I commend my soul;
I offer it to you with all the love of my
heart,
for I love you, Lord,
and so need to give myself,
to surrender myself into your hands,
without reserve,
and with boundless confidence,

For you are my Father.

Charles de Foucauld[7]

Waking Up to the Secret

In the Hindu mystic text, *Bhagavad Gita*, within the great mythic tale of India, the *Mahabharata*, the warrior Arjuna is brought on a spiritual journey to wake up to the reality of order as opposed to chaos. It's a journey that involves Dharma, Yoga, Nirvana, Devotion ...

Krishna, an incarnation of a god, urges Arjuna: "Fix your mind on Me, be devoted to Me, sacrifice to Me and worship Me, so you will come to Me, I promise you truly, for you are dear to Me."

Arjuna exclaims: "Destroyed is the confusion; and through your grace, O Changeless One, I understand: with doubts dispelled I shall do your word."[8] Jesus of Nazareth is not myth but the Word that became flesh.

The *Bhagavad Gita* seems an echo of the deep-down Truth that he is and shares with us.

Yes, there is peace in discovering

the secret presence of the One Jesus calls "Abba, Father."

Everything comes from him and is directed to him.

The Father wants

me to know him, Abba-Father.

Not as creature nor wretch, but as son, child.

Abba, Father ...

envelops me with his secret and infinite, loving and merciful presence.

So *all* my

asking, searching, knocking,
praying, suffering, building,
calling, questioning,
forgiving ...
everything is already and always of more con-
cern to him even than to myself.
The "Our Father" prayer
is truly summarized as "Our Father-Our Bread."
And so I can wake up each day,
look in the mirror and know
that I am known, loved and trusted.
There's peace in waking up to the secret
that dispels confusion and fear,
instilling confidence and strength.
"Come to Me and I will give you rest.
Trust in me ... Be not afraid"

Rediscovering the Father

Many years ago St. Cyprian commented that
we can't have God as Father
unless we have the Church as mother.
But in our times it has been said that there's a
   need today to recognize that
we can't know the Church as mother
unless we've known God as Father.

God is indeed "Father, "Abba."
The One who has given me life,
and a heart to love.
The One who has given me Jesus,
my brother along the journey.
The One who has given me Mary,
the Mother who is totally mine.
The One who has given me the Spirit,
friend of the soul.
The One who is at the beginning
of each of the Our Father petitions.
The One who is the root of All,
silent, discreet, Love,
immense Love
who accompanies each moment with his loving
   care.
Nothing is outside his furnace of love.
Good news, bad news,
All has its place in his plan.
Yes, to always believe in Love — not just sometimes but always.
"Cast all your anxiety onto the Father because he
   cares for you" (see 1 Pet 5:7).

Be a Father

It is often observed that our society has become father-less. Psychologically, socially and culturally what fathers traditionally stood for — authority, rule, stability — is rejected.

And yet, the "Father" is still yearned for.

How can I give the "father" to so many who cry out for one?

Recently I heard one priest say of another that he was a great priest not because he was a father figure but because in his life he showed Jesus, the Son. It was how he himself lived as a son, as Jesus, that put people, almost without realizing it, in relationship with God the Father.

Maybe that's it. In our world we need fathers who are fellow sons and daughters showing us *the* Father.

Jesus himself said there is only one Father.

The world needs sons and daughters who are simple, transparent and free. People like that know how to be big, strong and generous friends. As such they carry out the task of fathers and guides when asked.

What matters, then, is to look always to the One Father of many sons and daughters. And so to see all as children of the one Father and so brothers and sisters.

Saying "Thanks" with our Memory

Thankfulness is an attitude to be cultivated
in all dimensions of our lives.
It is certainly courteous to say "thanks" when a
  good deed has been done.
To recognize in my day to day life that I owe so
  much to those around me is important.
And that includes gratitude to those present to
  me though I do not notice them —
those who have constructed the building I live in,
put down the stone footpath tiles I walk on, work
in the city services that keep civic society going,
those who have made food deliveries by night to
the shops, those of former generations who did
their part in building up the society-home in
which we now live.
But I also need to say "thanks" for all the times
the Invisible One, God, has been present in my
life, coming to my aid, lifting me out of danger,
helping me.
Yes, it's good to pause now and then and say
"thanks" *with my memory*, to re-live the times
when troubles, problems and difficult situations
arose and God intervened.
Perhaps I hardly noted it at the time but circumstances worked out, things got resolved, problems got sorted.
But there is a temptation: why do I have to see
it as God's doing? Might it be only the natural
course of things?

Perhaps.

But perhaps, too, there is the providential hand of God behind it.

So why not try and go down memory lane with an attitude of gratitude and imagine life as if he has been present.

And give thanks.

Of course, in doing this, I might discover pain in the fragments of suffering that still linger from certain situations not yet fully resolved.

Wounds may heal but scars often remain.

But, no matter, I will try to give thanks with my memory.

God has been there, behind it all, even when he might have seemed to be absent. God has been at work in my life and in the lives of others.

I accept the invitation to travel along memory lane, and with the inner sense of the soul, tasting, feeling and seeing things with gratitude.

Doing Our Calculations in God

Every now and then
a situation arises that's like
entering a dark tunnel,
leading to a very narrow door.
I find myself hemmed in.
Which way should I go?
What am I to do?
How am I to manage?
What is the will of God for me?
I don't know.
I can't know.
I doubt what I know,
I have scruples about what I do know ...

On these occasions, what should I do?
Don't waste time.
From the best of my ability,
choose a way.
Cast the rest onto God.
Do my calculations in God.
If it's a wrong choice,
let circumstances show me the right way.
Go ahead,
through the narrow door.

Perhaps even to the very end, I will be
not sure, not knowing, not clear,
but trusting, entrusting and believing things
    will be resolved.
I'll pass through that narrow door.
Doubt will seem a mirage.
A new day will dawn.

3

The Unique Plan
for Each of Us

God has Created Me to Do Him Some Definite Service

*God has created me to do Him some
 definite service;
He has committed some work to me
which He has not committed to another.
I have my mission — I never may know
 it in this life,
but I shall be told it in the next.
Somehow I am necessary for His
 purposes ...
I have a part in this great work;
I am a link in a chain, a bond of
 connection between persons.
He has not created me for naught. I
 shall do good, I shall do His work;
I shall be an angel of peace, a preacher
 of truth in my own place, while not
 intending it,
if I do but keep His commandments
and serve Him in my calling.
Therefore I will trust Him.
Whatever, wherever I am,
I can never be thrown away.
If I am in sickness, my sickness may
 serve Him;
in perplexity, my perplexity may serve
 Him;*

*if I am in sorrow, my sorrow may serve
  Him.
My sickness, or perplexity, or sorrow
  may be
necessary causes of some great end,
which is quite beyond us.
He does nothing in vain; He may
  prolong my life,
He may shorten it;
He knows what He is about.
He may take away my friends,
He may throw me among strangers,
He may make me feel desolate,
make my spirits sink, hide the future
  from me—
still He knows what He is about....
Let me be Thy blind instrument. I ask
  not to see—
I ask not to know—I ask simply to be
  used.*

John Henry Newman[9]

"Yes" as Today's Guiding Word

A day ahead of me
to say "yes" —

> "yes" to those tasks that await me
> "yes" to the neighbors I will meet
> "yes" to accepting personal limits I'll
> encounter
> "yes" even when, because it is the right
> thing to do, I have to say "no" (which
> will be a "yes" to God or "yes" to
> love of my neighbor for God)
> "yes" to those moments of tension when I
> feel there's too much going on
> "yes" to that conversation that I'm
> nervous about
> "yes" to that "no" I need to say when
> faced with inner temptations of
> thought or of deed.
> "yes" to the difficulties
> "yes" said deep within me, hidden but
> clear in its intimacy,
> "yes" I want to love, and to love you I only
> have today, now.

Yes.

Celebrate

There is a deep-down point,
a hidden recess of the soul,
a center point
where, silently, discretely we can say our "yes"
to the God who has come among us in Jesus
  Christ.
The humanized God, the God with a human face.
The God who has made suffering, darkness and
  adversity his own.
So often he appears when I seem least inclined
to see him — times of perplexity and worry, dis-
couragement, neglect or fear, moments of failure
and confusion — in myself and in others.
But these are my opportunities to renew that
"yes" to him coming now in that way, precisely in
that very aspect that I'd love to banish.
To welcome him in that way is an effort, but
  God's help is available ...
And it's a healthy thing to do so.
What's more, as I do so,
 deep down I can "celebrate" his coming.
Not as an act of exuberance or superficial festiv-
ity, but rather as a determined act of the will: "if
you want it, I want it"; I celebrate your coming.
You are mine and I am yours.

A Criterion to Help

In the swirl of things to do,
A desire is there:
To do the good God wants
To not do the good God does not want.
I want to be in the place God wants me to be.
But the question arises:
Do I really need to do this or that?
Or, more precisely,
How do I know which good thing to do?
The right place to be?
There is a criterion to help:
Is it really love?
Does it build communion with God and with
others?
Is what I am doing and where I am right now
"rooted and grounded" in love (Eph 3:17)?

St. Augustine tells me as much:

> Once for all, then, a brief precept is given to
> you: Love, and do what you want. If you are
> silent, be silent with love; if you cry out, cry
> out with love; if you chastise, chastise with
> love; if you spare, spare with love. The root
> of love must be within; nothing but good can
> come forth from this root.[10]

Gaeta, Christmas 1988

It was most likely the last Christmas dinner for Don Cosimino, as his parishioners so affection-ately called him.

His cancer had now spread and conquered.

That Christmas morning had already usurped
what little energy he had.

He had invited people to imagine briefly where they might be in the original Christmas scene ...

But now it was dinner time.

So three together sit around the table with
Cosimino

in the simple Italian parish house,

trying their best to be "upbeat."

Just as they start into the pasta dish, a knock on
the door.

One of the three advances, wondering who could
be calling at this time on Christmas day.

Then the jolt. Before him stands a disheveled beggar, with a bushy beard, a true vagabond. He is looking for Don Cosimino.

And from within Cosimino hears and calls the
beggar by name, inviting him in.

He sits at table and the red sauce soon creams
his bushy beard in patches.

Could this be for real? On this Christmas day?

But the conversation opens up with Don
Cosimino mustering all his energy.

Banter, good humor, fun.

But then, Cosimino's one liner:

"You know you have a wife and children ... Think of them this Christmas ..."

Tears.

The beggar rises from the table and shuffles towards Cosimino, takes his hand and kisses it affectionately.

"You're the only one who tells me the truth. And with love. You're my true friend. *Grazie*, Don Cosimino."

More tears, gentle warmth, a moment of silence.

And the guest leaves.

Months later when news of Cosimino's death arrived,

it is also reported that a man spent hours in vigil outside the hospital in prayer.

That Christmas scene came back into the mind's eye,

together with its many lessons of Love that is true

and of Truth that is love.

Strange — But It All Fits In

It's strange to think that when writing his Gospel, Matthew should have listed so many names right at the beginning of the "Good News" he wanted to tell.

Perez, Tamar, Manasseh, Eleazar, Rahab, Judah, Uriah, Jechoniah ...

So many names.

Not all perfect people!

And many hidden reminders of tough times:

Judah and his brothers who sold Joseph their brother into slavery,

Rahab the prostitute in Jericho,

the adulterous David who arranged the killing of Uriah,

Jechoniah, who was king at the deportation of the people to Babylon.

Yet, Matthew pulls it all together at the end of his genealogy, showing there was a plan in it all: "so all the generations from Abraham to David are fourteen generations; and from David to the deportation to Babylon, fourteen generations; and from the deportation to Babylon to the Messiah, fourteen generations" (Mt 1:17).

As if to say to me too:

"Look back, the threads of life are like the back of a piece of needlework. At times they seem to be knotted, messy, not clear. But look again at the design from the front — as God sees it: there is a plan."

4

At the End
only Love Remains

I Have Finally Found
My Vocation —
My Vocation is Love

Without becoming discouraged, I continued my reading, and this sentence gave me relief: "Now eagerly desire the greater gifts. And yet I will show you the most excellent way" (1 Cor 12:31). And the Apostle explains how the most perfect gifts are nothing without Love ... and that Charity is the excellent way that leads surely to God. Finally I had found rest. Considering the mystical body of the Church, I had not recognized myself in any of the members described by St. Paul, or rather, I wanted to recognize myself in all of them.... Charity gave me the key to my vocation.... I understood that the Church had a heart, and that this heart was burning with Love. I understood that Love alone can cause the members of the Church to act. If Love were to be extinguished, the Apostles would no longer preach the gospel, the Martyrs would refuse to shed their blood.... I understood that Love contains all the Vocations, that Love is all, that it embraces all times and all places ... in a word, that it is Everlasting! Then in the excess of my delirious joy, I cried out, "Oh Jesus, my Love ... I have finally found my vocation: My vocation is Love!... Yes, I have found my place in the Church.... In the Heart of the Church, my Mother, I will be Love.... That way I will be everything ... that way my dream will become a reality!!!

Thérèse of Lisieux[11]

The Art of Loving

There is a new sense of the value of true love today. It has been said that society's ills aren't due so much to a lack of resources but rather to the lack of true relationships of love between individuals, peoples and nations.

Erich Fromm wrote on the need to learn the "art of loving," commenting on how "... people in our culture try so rarely to learn this art.... In spite of the deep-seated craving for love, almost everything else is considered to be more important than love: success, prestige, money, power — almost all our energy is used for the learning of how to achieve these aims, and almost none to learn the art of loving."[12]

For his part, in 2000 the then Cardinal Ratzinger observed that as people search for happiness, what they are looking for is someone to teach them the art of living, the art that Jesus taught.

Chiara Lubich too believes we discover this art of living and loving in the Gospel:

◇ *be the first to love (don't wait for others to love you);*

◇ *love your neighbor as yourself (that gives a balanced measure);*

◇ *love your enemy (trying to see things from their point of view helps!)*

◇ *and love one another (what Jesus calls "his" and "new" commandment).*

Love "Hurts" and Justice "Costs"

Mother Teresa used to say love is not love unless it "hurts." That's the barometer. It's so easy for timidity to cause me to step back before the hurt part. And so, for instance, I see someone walking out of a building to her car in the lashing rain, using a crutch. Her journey is short, but it occurs to me to get an umbrella and accompany her out...but then the timid thought: "well, it's only a short trip, she'll do without it ..." But that "love till it hurts ..." gives the measure, so I go get the umbrella, walk her out to the car. She's pleased, as is her mother who has come to meet her.

But love also means acting justly. That also costs. Catherine of Siena's words cut straight to the heart:

> When one is in charge, one often fails in true justice. And this is the reason: one is afraid of losing one's status, so in order not to displease others, one keeps covering and hiding their wrong-doing, smearing ointment on a wound which at the time needs to be cauterized. Alas, how sad I feel when those who should use the flame of divine charity to burn out crime by holy punishment and correction, administered in true justice, flatter others and pretend not to see their wrong-doing. They behave in this way toward those whom they think may harm their position.

But toward the poor who seem insignificant and whom they do not fear, they display tremendous enthusiasm for 'justice' and, showing neither mercy nor compassion, they exact harsh punishments for small faults.[13]

What Have I *Lived* Today?

As I look back on the day, I ask myself "What have I *lived* today?"
It's *the* question.
St. John of the Cross once wrote:
at the end of our lives we'll be judged on love.
There's no shortage of ways to love! And when my imagination needs prompting, there's the seven corporal works of mercy for starters:

◊ *feed the hungry, give drink to the thirsty, clothe the naked,*

◊ *shelter the homeless, visit the sick, visit the imprisoned, bury the dead.*

The seven spiritual works of mercy remind me that love is not only about doing "external" activities. Love is to:

◊ *counsel the doubtful, instruct the ignorant, admonish sinners;*

◊ *comfort the afflicted, forgive offenses;*

◊ *bear wrongs patiently, pray for the living and the dead.*

But the question always comes back to the basic one:
How much love have I put in to the day?

Love in all its colors —

- ◇ *humor when tensions arise over small issues,*

- ◇ *generously sharing gifts received,*

- ◇ *attending to doing little things well,*

- ◇ *approaching others with a smile,*

- ◇ *speaking, serving, doing, waiting*

— all out of love.
My great chance is to "live" life,
not simply to let it slide by.

Three Ways to Protest

When faced with what we find in any way wrong or objectionable or lamentable, we can adopt three attitudes:

The first is to go head-on and confront the person or body or institution concerned directly. It's the way of immediate opposition and clamor, criticism and truth. It has the beauty of being direct. Sometimes this might be necessary.

The second is to retreat into silence and not engage. This can be the way of virtuous long-suffering endurance. Those who protest in this manner are voting with their feet, as it were. It is protest in the form of silent withdrawal. At times it too has its place, though it risks becoming suppressed rage, or avoidance of the issue, or simply sinking into indifference, washing one's hands of the whole situation.

A third is to start out with a new proposal. This is the way of historical patience, knowing what can be changed and what cannot. It is protest in the most intelligent manner — start a new life-giving way. Build up something new — not out of violent opposition or self-righteousness or superiority, but simply because it is the right thing to do, the intelligent way to protest, perhaps slower but a surer way forward. Remake the broken mold so that the protest will last.

> They are like trees planted by streams of water, which yield their fruit in its season, and their leaves do not wither (Ps 1:3).

The Present Moment —
the Refining Tool of Love

To live the present moment
solemnly,
that is,

> not being in a rush
> doing things well
> paying attention to people
> casting away useless thoughts
> driving carefully
> putting up with little adversities
> offering everything, both bad and good
> reaching out
> praying more from the heart
> keeping inner freedom
> curbing sentiments of annoyance
> not postponing unpleasant tasks
> choosing words more carefully

depending on the "actual grace"
of each moment.

The present moment, when lived well, out of love
for my neighbor,
is like a fine chisel that shapes my life.
Yes, the present moment,
so much needed ...
and when lived, it brings deep satisfaction.

For everything there is a season, and a
> *time for every matter under heaven:*
a time to be born, and a time to die;
a time to plant, and a time to pluck up
> *what is planted;*
a time to kill, and a time to heal;
a time to break down, and a time to
> *build up;*
a time to weep, and a time to laugh;
a time to mourn, and a time to dance;
a time to throw away stones, and a time
> *to gather stones together;*
a time to embrace, and a time to refrain
> *from embracing;*
a time to seek, and a time to lose;
a time to keep, and a time to throw
> *away;*
a time to tear, and a time to sew;
a time to keep silence, and a time to
> *speak;*
a time to love, and a time to hate;
a time for war, and a time for peace.

(Eccl 3:1-8).

5

Keep Going Ahead

Don't Write Me Off

The Word became flesh.
The Word became heart.
God accepted a heart.
God's heart beats
in the countless millions
of human hearts.
Since then
we are able to know
what dwells in the heart of humanity,
because God who knows everything
wanted to be close to everything.
Not only did he want to know
what is in the heart of humanity —
he also wanted to experience it.
What is in our heart
may be troubled and disturbed,
but there is in it
always a longing
for the answer "yes" —
"Don't write me off!" —
"Forgive me!" —
"Give me another chance!" —
"Accept me!"
And there is even more than this
in every heart —
an even deeper mystery.
It is not just a longing —

it is reality.
Every heart is a heart that is loved.
For every human heart
is worth God's own heart
and God has offered himself up
for every human being.

Bishop Klaus Hemmerle[14]

Always Begin Again

It's morning.
A new day opens up for me.
Forget yesterday, try to see each person new.
Begin again.

As the day proceeds,
A memory comes back that disturbs.
Fling it into God's mercy.
Begin again.
A judgment rises in the heart against someone,
Cast it aside.
Begin again.
A word spoken in haste.
Say sorry and
Begin again.
A silly gaffe.
Don't analyse.
Begin again.

As the day draws to a close,
A disappointing result.
Don't try to over-analyse.
Begin again.
Another occasion of being let down.
Don't give in to resentment.
Begin again.
Always begin again.

St Bernard reminds us wisely: there is no standing still in the spiritual life. Those who do not go forward, go backwards.

Rectifying Intention

Throughout the day
I need to rectify intentions.
Keep the compass focused.
Is what I am doing *love*?
Is what I propose to do *love*?
All the rest is vanity of vanity.
So away with vain thoughts and useless inner
    monologues
justifying my opinions, viewpoints and proposals.
Bring myself back to the true direction:
love, relationships of truth and sincerity.
Rectify my intentions,
Five, ten, twenty times a day.

Along life's journey,
the sacrament of Reconciliation provides solemn
    moments
to rectify my intentions,
and to set the compass in the right direction
    again.
Because in this sacrament, visible sign of invis-
    ible reality,
I meet him who is the Way, the Truth and the
    Life.
He takes what is mine (sinfulness) and gives me
what is his, the Holy Spirit, the One who makes
all things new.

St. Benedict's Wise Counsel

I need to keep St. Benedict's wise counsel on the three degrees of humility before me always:
first of all, to *accept* humiliations when they come our way (failure or misunderstanding),
secondly to *love* them (saying to myself that God is working through this)
and the third to *prefer* them (a heroic act of the will!).

No to Murmuring

With the slavery of Egypt behind them,
the community of Israel went out
celebrating and singing.
But soon they entered the desert wilderness
grumbling and murmuring:
"Would it not be better to go back?"
"Would that we had died in the land of Egypt!"
Even when they had glimpsed the land of milk
    and honey
their murmuring could still be heard.

Murmuring can take hold so easily!

And yet God is always at work doing new things,
if only I open my eyes to see them and mouth to
speak of them:

> "I am about to do a new thing; now it springs
> forth, do you not perceive it?" (Is 43:19).

Saying Goodbye

The moments in life when we have to say "good-bye" are never easy, be it leaving someone we love, changing jobs, grieving a deceased.
Our memories record good times and kindness-es, warm words and affections.
But then too, in moving on, regrets, words not said, tasks not completed, jobs half-done, rela-tionships not built up, timidity in outreach.
It's the grain of wheat falling to the ground
in the hope that in time, there'll be new growth.
Then a thought consoles me:
"I may be unfaithful, but Jesus in me is always faithful."
He has made his own
all those moments wasted,
those opportunities lost,
those words that could have been said but weren't.
He has taken them all onto himself and trans-formed them into himself.
And he is always faithful.
This is consoling.
He-in-me has always loved.

6

We Go to God Together

Spirituality of Communion

To make the Church the home and school of communion: that is the great challenge facing us in the millennium which is now beginning, if we wish to be faithful to God's plan and respond to the world's deepest yearnings. But what does this mean in practice? Here too, our thoughts could run immediately to activities to be undertaken, but that would not be the right impulse to follow.

Before making practical plans, we need to promote a spirituality of communion.... A spirituality of communion indicates above all the heart's contemplation of the mystery of the Trinity dwelling in us, and whose light we must also be able to see shining on the face of our brothers and sisters around us. A spirituality of communion also means an ability to think of our brothers and sisters as "those who are a part of me." This makes us able to share their joys and sufferings, to sense their desires and attend to their needs, to offer them deep and genuine friendship.

A spirituality of communion implies also the ability to see what is positive in others, to welcome it and prize it as a gift from

God: not only as a gift for the brother or sister who has received it directly, but also as a "gift for me." A spirituality of communion means, finally, to know how to "make room" for our brothers and sisters, bearing "each other's burden" (Gal 6:2) and resisting the selfish temptations which constantly beset us and provoke competition, careerism, distrust and jealousy.

Blessed John Paul II[15]

Supernaturalize

What is the measure of a good relationship?
When we love one another.
And that means a love with all its nuances of vigilance and listening, creativity and patience, initiative and celebration, kindness and hope ...
But how can I live these virtues?
By letting Jesus live in me.
Then relationships become *Jesus to Jesus*.
Jesus in me loves Jesus in you and vice versa.
And for that to happen each of us needs to be "nothing,"
a nothingness of love that lets the Spirit work,
forming Jesus in me, Jesus in you, and Jesus among us.

A Christian Is ...

A Christian is one who has discovered that all of
  humanity is one and lives that out.

One because the mystical body of Jesus Christ
in some way embraces every man, woman and
child, past, present and future.

So others are not simply outside me. I am in
  them and they are in me.

So mine are the joys and sufferings of others.
  And theirs mine.

This explains why Pope Paul VI could say: no
  one is a stranger to me.

But how much must I change my mentality to let
  this reality of unity explode into life among
  us!

Every encounter is a chance for it to happen.

There's only one condition. Like the negative and
positive of an electric current, each of us needs
to know how to play the game of being "full" and
being "empty" in our talking and sharing, our
planning and loving, so that the current of unity
passes between us.

But it is worth it.

In true unity each of us finds our fullest and
  unique realization.

Because when there is unity, there is God.

And God expresses who I am.

After all, He has created me, and each and every
person, as a unique word that he has wanted to
say from all eternity.

"We Must Remain United" — A Refrain from Burundi

The devastating fighting of the civil war had finally arrived.

The enmity between Hutu and Tutsi was about to descend upon this group of teenagers.

Terrified, the seminarians in Buta prepare:

"We must remain united," they declare to one another.

At 5:00 am, the rebels break in: "Hutu on one side and Tutsi on the other!"

But the young men refuse to divide.

Suddenly, a massive explosion.

More than thirty die instantly.

The rebels continue to shoot, even among the dead ...

In the middle of this hell, a new declaration is voiced: "Forgive them for they do not know what they are doing."

Years have gone by. But the testimony of these "martyrs of unity" continues. Their word lives on.

A Mexican Parable: "The Other is Another Me"

Two boys growing up side by side in a small Mexican town, beautiful but desperately poor.
A new school gives a new chance.
Education, learning, example.
Then the final exam and the ticket to a new life.
The teachers' assessment is that the two boys have particular promise.
A scholarship should be found.
Eventually one is,
And the teachers opt for one of those boys whose mother is ill and whose father has died.
Delight, celebration, success.
Who knows what it would mean for his future life?
But then two days later he's back:
"I've come to say I want you to give the scholarship to the other guy." He explains he had found a simple job that would cover basic expenses and even manage the treatment for his mother.
He's asked, "But why give away this opportunity? It's such a chance for you." His swift reply: "What I've learned here is that the other is another me."

Visiting Dachau

Lighting the candles at a simple "Shabbat"
    ceremony
in the house near Augsburg,
two rabbis from America
welcome their Catholic friends.
The Exodus story is recalled
as a *now* event: "This is our story."
We are part of their Shabbat.
Mindful of parents and relatives
who had left Germany in dark circumstances
or been killed, the rabbis speak of faith.
Two days later, we visit Dachau together.
The dreadful gate with its inscription, "Arbeit
    macht frei"
[work sets you free]
opens before us the gruesome reminders of the
    war's horrors —
reconstructed barracks and prisoner bunks, dis-
    plays of history of the camp and crematoria.
Here so many Jews died from
starvation and weariness, typhus and executions.
Germans, Russians and French, Polish,
Yugoslavs and Czechs ...
Politicians and writers, royalty and freedom
    fighters.
Jews, many, many Jews.
And Catholic priests too.
As we roam around,
few words, much feeling.
On the silence God is speaking.

When the time comes to leave,
Rabbi Michael suggests we recite the Our Father
     prayer.
Two rabbis and a Catholic priest.
Joining hands, the words bind us deeply.
Afterwards we speak of a reconciling effect.
Yes, belief in *"Our* Father" heals.
One Father.
We are all brothers and sisters.
Let's witness to the living liturgy of reconciliation.
True freedom.

7

The Adventure of the Word

Are We Pervaded by the Word of God?

The disciples are thus drawn deep within God by being immersed in the word of God. The word of God is, so to speak, the bath which purifies them, the creative power which transforms them into God's own being. So then, how do things stand in our own lives? Are we truly pervaded by the word of God? Is that word truly the nourishment we live by, even more than bread and the things of this world? Do we really know that word? Do we love it? Are we deeply engaged with this word to the point that it really leaves a mark on our lives and shapes our thinking? Or is it rather the case that our thinking is constantly being shaped by all the things that others say and do? Aren't prevailing opinions the criterion by which we all too often measure ourselves? Do we not perhaps remain, when all is said and done, mired in the superficiality in which people today are generally caught up? Do we allow ourselves truly to be deeply purified by the word of God?

Benedict XVI[16]

If You Say So ... On Your Word

Peter, a fisherman, had finished his day's work, exhausted by his lack of success. He had tried but to no avail! Along comes a man who encourages him to give it another go. Peter's response is quite natural: "Look, I know how things are, it's pointless to try again especially when the daytime is the wrong time for fishing!" There was little reason to try. And yet Peter decides to start again from scratch: "If you say so." "On your word ..."

Peter abandons himself and his own way of seeing things to the word of the One who is Life. Far from any immature dependency, or making things easier for himself by empty-minded unenthusiastic resignation, Peter gets back to work. And the unexpected happens. A real miracle catch!

But even more, Peter suddenly realizes the power and greatness of Jesus and his words. And he also notices how different we are from God.

How great God is and how small, sinful and limited we are! Peter could easily have ended up stuck in a rut thinking about this, but Jesus tells him: "Don't be afraid" as if to say: "Now you realize that on your own you can do nothing; God can do everything. But I am the one sending you out again, don't trust yourself, trust me." And Peter becomes a bearer of a new dimension of life, a new fire, a new discovery of God and his word.

The Synagogue Museum in Buenos Aires

On the wall in the Jewish Museum in Buenos
  Aires
there's a picture of a man rejoicing.
The guide explains it's an expression of the joy of
  the conclusion of *Simchat Torah*.[17]
Rejoicing at the gift of the Word. Such joy that
the man looks almost intoxicated, beyond him-
self in glee, over the moon, exuberant.
Yes, a reminder — to rejoice in the gift of the
  Word.

The Word of God was there in the very beginning:

◇ *Enjoy its evidence in all of creation.*

The Word of God holds all things in being:

◇ *Enjoy the security of knowing its order
  beneath our world.*

The Word of God is alive and active:

◇ *Enjoy the chance to discern its traces in
  the world.*

The Word of God is Incarnate:

◇ *Enjoy knowing him. He has come for
  me.*

The Word of God has been written down:

◇ *Enjoy the possibility of reading and
  living it.*

The Word of God dwells among us:

◊ *Enjoy his presence among us when we are united in mutual love.*

Each of us is a word of God to be spoken to the world

◊ *Enjoy uttering that word with our life.*

Be Happy

The last words of the young Blessed Chiara Luce Badano to her mother were: "Be happy, because I am."

Beatitude (happiness) is everyone's deepest desire.

To be able to reach the end of our life saying "I am happy" is a gift worth striving for.

But who will show the pathway of happiness?

The One who said he had come to bring Good News and life, liberation, sight and healing.

When Chiara Luce was nine, she felt she had to really begin to take her relationship with him much more seriously.

And so she launched out in a divine adventure that was to conclude within ten years — the journey of living in happiness, being faithful to the life of the Gospel, the Good News that is not just for our personal consolation or meditation, but for bringing about a new world, a world where people see each other new, seeing Jesus in the poor, the outcast, the jeering, the young.

It was Chiara Luce's way, the way that led to happiness.

The Pelican Principle

Dissatisfaction arises in wanting to communicate to others important truths, insights and discoveries ... but my words seem so hollow.

It's then that the Pelican principle comes back to mind.

A pelican is said to feed its young with its own blood.

So, when I want to share truth, light and wisdom, it's important to communicate it as life.

What has been *lived* speaks and reaches the inner chords of the heart, and this is convincing.

There are many preachers in the world.

But what the world needs especially today is witnesses,

those who live the Pelican principle,

feeding others with truth by sharing what they are living of that truth.

This always costs because it's a risk — giving away a piece of my very self.

But the communion of soul that it can establish is the premise for real communication.

Living the Word Together

"Create in me a pure heart, O God, and renew a
    steadfast spirit within me" (Ps 51:10 NIV).
These words express the heart's yearning for
    purity.
There is a source of purity — the Word.
Keeping the Word uppermost in my mind
can cleanse me of useless other words that can
    clutter the mind.
It provides hygiene for thought and soul.
But it's hard to live the Word on our own.
That's why it is a gift to have found others
with whom I can live the adventure of the Word
    together.
We become a reminder for each other, a stimulus,
    an encouragement.
Living the Word builds us up and creates
    community.

8

The *Why* That Answers All Our Questions

"I Know Only Christ and Christ Crucified"

*I have only one Spouse on earth: Jesus
     forsaken.*
I have no other God but him.
*In him there is the whole of paradise
     with the Trinity*
*and the whole of the earth with
     humanity.*
*Therefore what is <u>his</u> is mine, and
     nothing else.*
*And <u>his</u> is universal suffering, and
     therefore mine.*
*I will go through the world seeking it in
     every instant of my life.*
What hurts me is <u>mine</u>.
*Mine the suffering that grazes me in the
     present.*
Mine the suffering of the souls beside me
(that is my Jesus).
*Mine all that is not peace, not joy, not
     beautiful, not lovable, not serene,*
in a word, what is not paradise.
Because I too have <u>my</u> paradise,
but it is the one in my Spouse's heart.
I know no other.
*So it will be for the years I have left: a
     thirst for suffering,*
anguish, despair, separation, exile,

> *forsakenness, torment —*
> *for all that is him,*
> *and he is sin, hell.*
> *In this way*
> *<u>I will dry up</u> the waters of tribulation*
> *in many hearts nearby*
> *and, through communion*
> *with my almighty Spouse,*
> *in many far away.*
> *I shall pass as a fire*
> *that consumes all that must fall*
> *and <u>leaves standing only</u> the truth.*
> *But it is necessary to be <u>like</u> him:*
> *to be him in the present moment of life.*

Chiara Lubich[18]

We can walk as much as we want, we can build many things, but if we do not profess Jesus Christ, things go wrong. We may become a charitable NGO, but not the Church, the Bride of the Lord. When we are not walking, we stop moving. When we are not building on the stones, what happens? The same thing that happens to children on the beach when they build sandcastles: everything is swept away, there is no solidity ... When we journey without the Cross, when we build without the Cross, when we pro-fess Christ without the Cross, we are not disciples of the Lord, we are worldly: we may be bishops, priests, cardinals, popes, but not disciples of the Lord. My wish is that all of us, after these days of grace, will have the courage, yes, the courage, to walk in the presence of the Lord, with the Lord's Cross; to build the Church on the Lord's blood which was poured out on the Cross; and to profess the one glo-ry: Christ crucified. And in this way, the Church will go forward.

Pope Francis[19]

The Lightning Rod

A dark November day,
 entering the Church
I come before the tabernacle.
The situation is impossible.
No word is right.
Every suggestion seems wrong.
Confusion reigns.
The wound is deep.
Division all round.
Even hatred hits.
It's as if the situation has become like
a lightning rod attracting
the sharp, searing fulminations of pain, anger
    and rage ...
But then suddenly a thought —
You, Jesus, are that Lightning Rod!
You have taken onto yourself
the wounds, the division, the confusion,
the impossible, the lament , the "why" questions
so as to shelter, to heal, to unite ...
Yes, that's what counts:
to imitate you, lightning rod ...
mine the suffering of those beside me
mine the anger, confusion and rage
mine the questions
mine all that is not peace.
And so,
on that dark November day, a conviction stirs
    my soul:
In communion with You, I can do your work,

or better, it is no longer I in you but You at work in me.

> We are afflicted in every way, but not crushed; perplexed, but not driven to despair; persecuted, but not forsaken; struck down, but not destroyed; always carrying in the body the death of Jesus, so that the life of Jesus may also be made visible in our bodies. For while we live, we are always being given up to death for Jesus' sake, so that the life of Jesus may be made visible in our mortal flesh. So death is at work in us, but life in you (2 Cor 4:8-12).

Two Faces — Three Days

In the Pauline Chapel in the Vatican, two large canvasses painted by Michelangelo face one another, one depicting the crucifixion of Peter, the other Paul's Damascus experience.

The elderly Michelangelo shows us Peter being crucified, as is the tradition, upside down. He is surrounded by a hate-filled, venomous, condemning crowd. And Peter himself looks out at us almost despairingly saying, "What's going on? ... How has it come to this? ... Why? ... Will my death serve any purpose?"

Opposite him is Paul, fallen off a horse, thrown down and blinded. He has come to know the One who had said "Why are you persecuting me?" — the Risen Crucified Jesus. Momentarily he is blinded by the light that has overwhelmed him.

Two faces, one story. At times, I cannot see, or at least, I sense only the persistent question, "What's the point?" The "third day," the day that brings light can come unexpectedly and initially be blinding. In each case, however, it's a case of closing my eyes to one way of seeing things, opening to the newness that comes not of my own making or doing, or at the time I'd plan or want, but as a gift, the gift of light and life when and wherever the "third day" *God* wants, happens.

You Are There Playing Hide and Seek

In the sore tensions that arise —
    You are there
In the heated conversation that ends abruptly —
    You are there
In the rude interruption —
    You are there
In misunderstandings no matter how much we
try to explain to each other —
    You are there
In the nagging sense of dissatisfaction —
    You are there
In the dreadful inability to make oneself clear —
    You are there
In the outright rejection —
    You are there
In the sneering criticism —
    You are there
In the rejection —
    You are there
In the cavalier dismissal of what we each hold
dear —
    You are there
In the humiliating failure to persuade —
    You are there
In the dark space —
    You are there
In the smart remark —
    You are there

In the lack of feeling accepted —
    You are there.

Yes, it's you.
Jesus Crucified and Forsaken,
The One who has made his own all that divides
    and upsets,
all our "why" questions.

Yes, it's you,
playing hide and seek,
glimpsed in different guises.

Grant me the grace to
recognize you, love you, prefer you.

Is Everything Lovable?

Martin Luther, following on St. Augustine, wrote
that love makes the other lovable.
But is it true?
How can I love what appears to me as not lovable?
Not only persons who don't attract me but also
unlovable situations, human misery, frustrating
circumstances, humiliating events, threatening
prospects?
Beneath everything is the One who has entered
ahead of us into all of these situations — Jesus
Forsaken by All, the One who has made himself
pain, misery, frustration, humiliation, threat,
hurt, rejection...
So everything is a reflection of him, a presence
of him, an encounter with him.
To recognize him is to know the One who holds
the key of history.
And so, when my soul strives to "see" him in all
that seems unlovable, then I can say, "Yes, everything is lovable" even when it seems "horrible."
And, united with him in going out to love, even
the love of my small heart can make the apparently unlovable lovable.

Learning from the Eucharist

Sometimes in conversation we say, "I was eaten alive," meaning someone has reprimanded us severely. It's not pleasant, and we don't particularly relish the thought of it happening!

But there is a sense in which we can let ourselves voluntarily be "eaten alive." It's when we take our lead from the Eucharist. At the Last Supper, anticipating the total gift of himself on the Cross, Jesus made himself food for us. In his "love to the end," he gave and gave and gave ... to the point of letting himself become the bread from heaven to be "eaten" by us.

And so, we can learn from this.

We can let ourselves be "consumed" by our neighbors.
Yes, our giving has to reach this point.

Every time we participate in the celebration of the Mass, we not only celebrate the memorial of Jesus Christ's death on the Cross and resurrection. We also learn how to live "consumed" because, Thomas Aquinas has written, that there is not a single example of virtue that the Cross does not give us. "Do you seek an example of charity? 'There is no greater love than to give up one's life for those whom we love.' And Christ did it on the Cross ... Are you looking for an example of patience? The most perfect patience is found the Cross ... An example of humility? Look upon the Crucified One. An example of obedience? Follow him who made himself obedient to the Father even unto death ... An example of scorn for earthly things? Walk after him who is the King of Kings and Lord of Lords, in whom are found all the treasures of wisdom and who, nonetheless, appears naked on the Cross, an object of mockery ... put to death.[20]

9

Where Two or Three ...

A New Space of Life has Opened up for Us

Essential, then, is the fact that Jesus's Resurrection was not just about some deceased individual coming back to life at a certain point, but that an ontological leap occurred, one that touches being as such, opening up a dimension that affects us all, creating for all of us a new space of life, a new space of being in union with God.... In any case, it follows that the disciples did not feel abandoned. They do not consider Jesus to have disappeared far away into an inaccessible heaven. They are obviously convinced of a new presence of Jesus. They are certain...that he is now present to them in a new and powerful way. They know that "the right hand of God" to which he "has been exalted" includes a new manner of his presence; they know that he is now permanently among them, in the way that only God can be close to us.

The joy of the disciples after the "Ascension" corrects our image of this event. "Ascension" does not mean departure into a remote region of the cosmos but, rather, the continuing closeness that the disciples experience so strongly that it becomes a source of lasting joy ... Because Jesus is with the Father, he has not gone away but remains close to us. Now he is no longer in one particular place in the world as he had been before the "Ascension": now, through his power over space, he is present and accessible to all — throughout history and in every place.

Christ, at the Father's right hand, is not far away from us. At most we are far from him, but the path that joins us to one another is open. And this path is not a matter of space travel of a cosmic-geographical nature: it is the "space travel" of the heart, from the dimension of self-enclosed isolation to the new dimension of world-embracing divine love.

Benedict XVI[21]

The Risen Christ

When, through loving one another,
we allow the Risen Lord to be
present tangibly among us,
then everything takes on a new light.
With him among us,
there is ardor and enthusiasm,
zeal, peace and joy,
courage, resolution and inner peace.
Life seems to sprint ahead.
Every moment seems to become
an experience of being
in the eye of the storm of Love.
Yes, because whoever comes in contact with Him
comes into contact with Fire.
So, it's worth "forgetting myself"
and living transferred into my neighbor who,
if he or she reciprocates my love,
offers me the greatest gift of all —
the chance of letting a cell of the mystical body
explode into life.

I am the Holy One in your midst (Hos 11:9).

Preparing for Paradise

He had been a hard father; the sons were
   estranged.
But that final bonfire that is death has put things
   in perspective now.
Dying of cancer,
he decides to receive the sacraments.
But is that enough? His wife and daughter ask.
So they make a pact.
Let's surround him with such mutual love
that the sacraments will achieve their effects.
Because the Reality he will meet in the next life
   is Love.
The days pass.
The mother and daughter do their part.
One by one the sons come and are reconciled.
On that decisive Saturday evening, the last one
   enters,
the father smiles in recognition.
then minutes later life begins to fade from his
   gaunt face ravaged by illness.
At his death there is peace.
Yes, the pact of mutual love worked.
That "hard father" now reconciled
moves from the paradise of mutual love on earth
to the eternal paradise
where only love enters to meet Love
where each encounter will always be love.
where the Sun will shine for ever.

> You make him glad with the joy of your pres-
> ence (Ps 21:6).
> In Your light we see light (Ps 36:9).

Descartes' Act of Thanksgiving

It is said that when Descartes discovered his "I think therefore I am," he was immensely grateful. He affirmed, "And I realized that I must devote my life to cultivating reason and to revealing to mankind the truth with invincible proofs. And at once I resolved upon a pilgrimage to Loreto, to offer thanks at the shrine of the Virgin for thus delivering me from the evils and falsehoods in which hitherto I had found my contentment."[22]

Thinking is more than the calculation of 2 + 2 = 4.
It is more, as Václav Havel put it, than knowing the price of tomatoes.
It is about tuning into the Truth we are made for.

How are we to think?
In his Seventh Letter, Plato describes how dialogue and living together facilitate thinking: "suddenly a light, as it were, is kindled in one soul by a flame that leaps to it from another, and thereafter sustains itself."

The disciples on the road to Emmaus also discovered how to think:
It is a movement of exodus from partial viewpoints, in openness to the Easter Advent, the Word coming among us.
To live mutual love not only in deeds, but also with our mind, allows the Truth to inhabit our thinking with light.

Unity in Truth

The life of unity with one another is a daily conquest.
Its requirements are constant yet always new.
We are forever starting from scratch.
To sense Jesus among us we need to prepare the terrain:

◇ *loving moment by moment*

◇ *brushing away the dust that settles so easily in our relationships*

◇ *looking for ways to help one another practically*

◇ *overlooking those defects noticed for the umpteenth time*

◇ *renewing a pact of mercy among us — promising to see each other with new eyes — to be activated every morning*

◇ *living transparently in what we say and do*

◇ *speaking and acting with discretion and sensitivity*

◇ *finding the right moment to offer correction and advice*

◇ *spending time in "wasting" time with one another*

◇ *getting to understand where each other*

is coming from

◇ *being frank in what we have to tell one another*

◇ *communicating the life we have lived to keep Life alive among us*

◇ *guarding against idle gossip*

◇ *trusting each other*

◇ *having courage to confront obstacles that we discover*

◇ *enjoying the funny side of things*

◇ *laughing a lot*

◇ *keeping our group or community open, not closing in on ourselves*

◇ *sharing insights, discoveries and fruits of reading and thinking*

◇ *knowing how to "lose"*

◇ *resisting the temptation to judge*

◇ *waiting patiently but actively in love when unity is diminished*

◇ *silencing the creature within*

◇ *speaking so as to communicate*

◇ *loving to the end.*

Once the terrain is prepared, we've done "our" part.
Then we await the gift — the invisible but real presence of Him who is unity.

"Unity! Who could dare speak of it?
It is ineffable as God.
You feel it, see it, rejoice over it but ... it is ineffable!
All enjoy its presence, all suffer its absence.
It is peace, joy, love, ardor, and the spirit of heroism, of boundless generosity.
It is Jesus among us."[23]

Our Gift of Thanks to Nature

There are moments when a landscape suddenly strikes me — either for its beauty in the haze of an evening sun's glow that harmonizes everything, or for its wildness in a storm that causes the sea's white horses to fight, trees to rage and racing clouds to threaten, or for the night's sky that never ceases to fascinate. Nature's sheer being there reminds us how the world, our home, has been there millions of years before us and will probably be there long, long after us.

At moments such as these I would like to express the awe I sense. Also because the outer landscape so often expresses "the inscape," as Gerard Manly Hopkins put it, of the soul (individual and societal), with its moments of harmony and times of turbulence.

That's why it is good to have artists of every sort to help us express the deep down things evoked in us. As George Steiner puts it "it is the poet, the composer, the painter, it is the religious thinker and metaphysician when they give to their findings the persuasion of form, who instruct us that we are monads haunted by communion."[24]

If nature arouses in us moments of recognition of the something more to which we are called, we, for our part, can offer "brother sun, sister moon," that "something more" that expresses the relationship between the cosmos and God

— and that "something more" is the presence of Jesus among us.

He is the Word of God among us, the One in whom all has been created and redeemed and for whom all exists. What more can we offer in thanksgiving to creation that is our home than to allow Him, who is the Way, to become the Wayfarer among us in the world with its harmony, storms and sheer upward striving towards fulfillment. He is Ecology. He is Eternity. He is the New Heavens and the New Earth.

With Him among us, we begin to shape our home according to his measure, coloring the bits and pieces of our everyday world — from our economy to our recreation — with the dimensions of his love.

10

Taking Mary into our Home

In Praise of Mary

O Mary, artist of life, hail!
By recreating wholeness, you have
*   convulsed death itself.*
You have destroyed the serpent which,
*   blown up with pride,*
raised its outstretched neck to Eve.
You have trampled on it by giving birth
*   out of heaven*
to God's Son,
breathed into you by the Spirit of God.
O loveliest and most loving Mother, hail!
You have given forth into this world
*   your Son,*
sent from heaven and breathed into you
*   by the Spirit of God.*
Praised be the Father, the Son, and the
*   Holy Spirit.*
Breathed into you by the Holy Spirit.

Hildegard of Bingen[25]

She Searched for John, the One Recommended

At the foot of the Cross
Mary said a new "yes" to God.
She had totally centered her life on Jesus.
Now he was departing.
She stood motionless.
Emptiness, silence, loneliness.
What was she to do?
In the silence it became clear ...
"Woman, here is your son ..."
Let him go.
Now search for John,
the one "recommended" and entrusted to her by
    her son.
"And from that hour the disciple took her into his
own home."

Still today Mary searches for each person as that
    "John"
recommended to her by her Son.
Losing one form of maternity to take up another.
There is consolation in this thought: we have a
    mother in heaven.
But there is also a lesson.
Mary in her desolation at the foot of the Cross is
    a model.
I too can live like her:
seeing everyone as somebody "recommended,"
    entrusted to me.
And treat them accordingly.

To Lose

"You bring to heaven what you have lost in life" —
that's what someone I knew once said before
   dying.
It's a challenging phrase.
Yes, the Gospel says it too: those who lose their
   life find it.
How much there is to lose:
ideas, likes and dislikes,
habits, points of view and projects,
vices and attachments,
time, plans and reputation...

But losing seems so negative!
Is there a way of losing that is positive?

Perhaps it is to lose by giving,
that is, offer out of love my idea, my point of view,
   my project, my time ...
In losing by giving we move on in the great
   journey
from being isolated individuals to non-defensive
   persons.
The individual remains alone in a self-defined
   cocoon.
The person, losing, in giving, in relating
breaks out of that hard covering
and so is made universal,
opens more and more to everyone and so contains everyone.
Just like Adam and Eve in the original plan.
Just like Jesus and Mary at the Cross.

Espouse Wisdom

It is said that there is nothing more pleasing to God than people who live with wisdom.

Not the old head-on-young-shoulders wisdom

but that which comes from knowledge infused by love.

It doesn't come from cleverness or shrewdness or having a good take on things ...

The wisdom pleasing to God is gained not in books

but in the distillation of life's everyday ups and downs.

What matters is to "espouse" wisdom.

And so, I shall invite her in, ask her to make herself at home, listen to what she has to say, follow her lead, take up her suggestions, fall in love with her.

To "espouse" wisdom is the one thing necessary.

Mary knew that. We call her "Seat of Wisdom."

Mary and the Spirit

During the Second World War, the young Karol Wojtyła went through something of a faith crisis — in his life, would Mary detract from the place due to Jesus?

It was one of those questions the Holy Spirit puts into a heart because he wants to offer a response.

Karol discovered the answer to his question in Louis-Marie Grignion de Montfort's work, *True Devotion to the Blessed Virgin Mary*.

Mary is intimately linked to the Incarnation, the Outpouring of the Spirit, our sharing in God's Trinitarian life.

Reading this book became a truly "decisive turning-point" in his life.

Years later Karol Wojtyła still remembered carrying the book with him, even at the sodium factory.

Likewise the Irishman, Frank Duff, Founder of the Legion of Mary, in 1919 encountered Montfort's book that depicted Mary in "a devastatingly different dimension to what we were accustomed. The catechism had never shown us anything even remotely like that." [26]

It was like an electric shock in his life.

Montfort reminds us that when Mary is found in a person's life, the Holy Spirit rushes in.[27]

Mary is the mold that shapes us as Christians.

Mary Remembers

So often in tragic circumstances
I've seen how
it is consoling
simply to recall that
Mary does not forget us;
she remembers;
she's looking after us
even in the most apparently desperate situations.
The simple truth is that the words we repeat,
even only half-consciously,
do not fall on deaf ears: "Pray for us *now*...and at
   the *hour of our death*."
Yes. We have a mother in heaven. She hears these
   words.
And she remembers.
So even when I might forget Mary,
she does not fail to remember me.
Always.
As we go through life,
she makes a declaration: I am "totally yours."
Totally mine as mother and sister, advocate and
   refuge,
confidante of the soul, cause of joy.
So I can trust that "at the hour of my death"
she will be there, remembering even my perhaps
   long-forgotten petitions.
But why wait till the hour of death to develop my
relationship with her?
Even now, Mary, mother of unity, gently awaits
my heart's conversation.

"I am totally yours" ... "And I too, *totus tuus*."

11

Holy Spirit,
Friend of the Soul

Consuming Fire, Spirit of Love

O my God, Trinity whom I adore, help me to forget myself entirely that I may be established in You as still and as peaceful as if my soul were already in eternity. May nothing trouble my peace or make me leave You, O my Unchanging One, but may each minute carry me further into the depths of Your Mystery. Give peace to my soul; make it Your heaven, Your beloved dwelling and Your resting place....

O consuming Fire, Spirit of Love, "come upon me" and create in my soul a kind of incarnation of the Word: that I may be another humanity for Him in which He can renew His whole Mystery. And you, O Father, bend lovingly over Your poor little creature; "cover her with Your shadow," seeing her only the "Beloved in whom you are well pleased."

O my Three, my all...Immensity in which I lose myself, I surrender myself to You as Your prey. Bury Yourself in me that I may bury myself in You until I depart to contemplate in Your light the abyss of Your greatness.

Elizabeth of the Trinity[28]

A Birthday Resolve

Let me listen to your voice
and harden not my heart.
(Interiore hominis habitat veritas.)
Let me live within
where the Truth dwells.
Let me listen to your voice
and close not my heart to my brothers and sisters.
Let me live in mutual love,
so that the voice of Truth may be amplified.
Let Mary be Seat of Wisdom
as I take her into my home.

Yes, in the Spirit, heaven can be on earth
even as we make our way along the "valley of
tears."

And so we pray St. Augustine's words:[29]

Breathe in me, Spirit of God,
that I may think what is holy;
Drive me, Spirit of God,
that I may do what is holy;
draw me Spirit of God,
that I may love what is holy;
strengthen me, Spirit of God,
that I may preserve what is holy;
guard me, Spirit of God,
that I may never lose what is holy.

Ready to Change

It's easy to settle into the routine, the well-trust-
ed pattern.
I have "my" world with its familiar faces, defined
tasks, comfortable reference points.
But what if...I am asked to change, to go in another direction, to give up what I've been doing
and move into new fields of action?
The Spirit, wrote Irenaeus in the second century,
keeps the vessel of faith ever young.
And the Spirit is always active, rejuvenating...
if I allow this.
I need to be docile, ready to change everything at
the whisper of his voice.

Reparation

The word "reparation" is not appealing.
At least for many it smacks of another time —
long penances, harsh outlooks, severity.
The three children of Fatima, we are told, made
great reparation for the sins of the world.
And yet, now too, so much needs to be "repaired"
around us and within us.
I need to hear of reparation.
The legal world speaks today of reparative jus-
tice — the justice that repairs and heals.
But is there a way to live reparation spiritually?
Perhaps it is this:
To choose to follow more deeply
the One who has repaired all by his death on a
Cross.
To make reparation is to choose to follow him
with new decisiveness,
to follow him with all the love of my heart and
with courage right there within me and around
me where there is this need of reparation.

Martin Heidegger wrote that in the nocturnal
era of the world, the abyss must be recognized
and expressed right to its depths. But for that to
happen there needs to be people who reach the
abyss. Our times require people who have a new
look on life starting out from the abyss, or rather, from the experience of existential abyss that
Jesus went through. To start with him and from
him to see all things new with his eyes.

In his crucifixion, Jesus "expired" the Spirit (and
    the Spirit poured over humanity)
In our entering into the abyss with him, we too
    are given the chance to "expire" the Spirit
with him in today's world.
And so repair.
Living reparation.

Actual Grace

Edith Stein, the philosophy professor, visiting a
  colleague.
A simple circumstance.
Staying overnight she finds in her friend's house
  the autobiography of Teresa of Avila.
Just one simple book.
She spends the night reading the book and con-
  cludes she has to change her life completely.
A conversion when least expected.
Actual grace,
that is, a gift from God in real time!
God is always at work for my sanctification with
his interventions that actually work in each moment, situation and context.
If I am open.
How many examples of actual grace fall upon me
  every day
if I am in the right place to grasp them!
And each place and each moment is the right
  place
If I am open.
So, it's good to resolve to be attentive to "actual
  grace"
in the apparently coincidental, insignificant and
  trivial moments
as well as in the assistance to do the specific
  tasks life brings to me.
God is there, intervening.

"The word that came to Jeremiah from the
Lord: 'Come, go down to the potter's house,

and there I will let you hear my words.' So I went down to the potter's house, and there he was working at his wheel. The vessel he was making of clay was spoiled in the potter's hand, and he reworked it into another vessel, as seemed good to him.

Then the word of the Lord came to me: 'Can I not do with you, O house of Israel, just as this potter has done?' says the Lord. 'Just like the clay in the potter's hand, so are you in my hand, O house of Israel'" (Jer 18:1-6).

We Give What Is Ours and We Receive What Is His

To love God — the one thing necessary.
And one way of doing this one thing necessary is for me to "give" him all that happens to me throughout the day,
especially the boundary moments.

"I can't do that piece of work that is expected of me..." —
    I give it to you, Lord.

"I can't resolve that family situation that needs my help..." —
    I give it to you, Lord.

"There's that personal turmoil in my soul that's hounding me..." —
    I give it you, Lord.

"That person I find so hard to get on with...." —
    I give it to you, Lord.

"My inability to live love..." —
    I give it to you, Lord.

"Those moments of lack of faith" —
    I give them to you, Lord.

Yes, throughout the day, there are many moments when I can "give" to God.
Of course, God will not be outdone in giving.

If I offer him the boundary moments, he opens me to his infinite horizon.

If I hand over my sins, he showers upon me his mercy.

If I submit my fears, he instills his strength.

But it isn't just boundaries, sins and fears that I can surrender.

I remember Ignatius of Loyola's *Suscipe*:

> *Take, Lord, and receive my entire*
>   *liberty,*
> *my memory, my understanding and my*
>   *whole will.*
> *All that I am and all that I possess You*
>   *have given me.*
> *I surrender it all to You to be governed*
>   *according to Your will.*
> *Give me only Your love and Your grace;*
> *with these I will be rich enough,*
> *and will desire nothing more.*

Yes,

in carrying out the one thing necessary

I can offer God my "all" — my memory, mind, and will,

my talents, possibilities and potential.

I give what is mine, and he gives me what is his:
the seven gifts of the Spirit so necessary for life,

> to my searching, wisdom,
> to my analysis, understanding,
> to my decision-making, counsel,
> to my efforts, fortitude,
> to my quest for science, knowledge,

to my faltering reverence, piety.
to my desire for perseverance, fear of the Lord.

All of life's moments are opportunities provided by God to practice the culture of giving to him.

Give and gifts will be given to you.

This culture of giving to God can be lived out most clearly when I share with others. I journey to God with them. So a privatized spiritual asceticism is not enough. My brothers and sisters are the door through which I pass to give to God. The return may not be immediate but God always responds through brothers and sisters, perhaps when I least expect.

> Give, and it will be given to you. A good measure, pressed down, shaken together, running over, will be put into your lap; for the measure you give will be the measure you get back (Lk 6:38).

Come, Holy Spirit

Veni, Sancte Spiritus,
et emitte caelitus
lucis tuae radium.

The ancient Latin hymn to the Holy Spirit
is timeless in application.
How much the Holy Spirit is required in life!

Bend what is rigid,
Warm what is cold,
Guide what is astray.

Yes, we need to pray:

Come, Father of the poor
Come, giver of gifts
Come, light of our hearts.

It is necessary to invite the third Divine Person
to be:

Rest in labor,
Relief in oppressive heat,
Consolation in weeping

We can't do without the Spirit's work: *"Heal what*
is wounded."

It's easy to understand why the Orthodox
Ecumenical Patriarch Athenagoras often re-
peated that, "without the Spirit, God is far away,
Christ remains in the past, the Gospel is a dead
letter, the Church is a simple organization, authority a domination, mission a propaganda,

worship mere evocation, and Christian action a slave morality. But in the Spirit... the Risen Christ is present, the Gospel is the power of life, the Church signifies Trinitarian communion, authority is a liberating service, mission is a Pentecost, the liturgy is memorial and anticipation, human activity is deified."[30]

> *"Come, Holy Spirit, send forth the heavenly radiance of your light."*

Notes

1. See Chiara Lubich, *A New Way: The Spirituality of Unity* (New York: New City Press, 2006).

2. See Chiara Lubich, *Essential Writings: Spirituality, Dialogue, Culture* (New York: New City Press, 2007).

3. Jean Vanier, *Our Journey Home: Rediscovering a Common Humanity Beyond Our Differences* (Maryknoll, NY: Orbis, 1997), 171-72.

4. Sermo 1 in Nativitate Domini, 2.3: PL 54, 191-192.

5. Words attributed to William Booth and quoted in J. Evan Smith, *Booth the Beloved* (Oxford University Press, 1949), 123-24.

6. See Bonaventure, *Journey of the Mind into God* (Indianapolis,IN: Hackett Pub. Co.,1993), Prologue, n.3.

7. In Teresa de Bertodano, ed., *The Book of Catholic Wisdom: 2000 Years of Spiritual Writing* (Chicago: Loyola Press, 2001), 24-25.

8. 18: 65 and 73.

9. *Meditations and Devotions of the Late Cardinal Newman* (New York: Longmans, Green and CO., 1907), Hope in God— Creator, March 7, 1848.

10. Augustine, *Homilies on the First Epistle of John* (New York: New City Press, 2008), 110.

11. *The Story of a Soul* (New York: Doubleday, 1957), 161.

12. Erich Fromm, *The Art of Loving* (London: Unwin Paperbacks, 1975), 12.

13. Catherine of Siena, "If you want to rule well, practice justice" (Letter, 268) in Mary O'Driscoll, *Catherine of Siena: Passion for the Truth Compassion for Humanity* (New York: New City Press, 2008), 41-43, here 41.

14. This meditation by Klaus Hemmerle, the late Bishop of Aachen, Germany, is found in *They Laid Him in a Manger: A Way to the Heart of Christmas* (London: New City, 1990), 16-17.

15. Pope John Paul II, Apostolic Letter at the beginning of the new millennium, *Novo Millennio Ineunte* (6 January 2001), n. 43.

16. Benedict XVI, *Chrism Mass,* 9 April 2009.

17. Conclusion of the annual Torah reading cycle involving dancing in synagogue as all the Torah scrolls are carried around in seven circuits.

18. Chiara Lubich, *Essential Writings: Spirituality, Dialogue, Culture* (New York: New City Press, 2007), 95.

19. To Cardinals, March 14, 2013.

20. *Expositio in Symbolum* 4, nn. 919-24 quoted in Jean-Pierre Torrell, *Saint Thomas Aquinas.* Volume 2: *Spiritual Master.* Trans. By Robert Royal (Washington, D.C.: Catholic University of America Press, 2003), 120.

21. See Joseph Ratzinger/ Benedict XVI, *Jesus of Nazareth,* Part Two: *Holy Week: From the Entrance into Jerusalem to the Resurrection* (San Francisco: Ignatius Press, 2011), 274, 281, 284, 286.

22. *Discourse on Malady,* attributed to Rene Descartes, edited by Jürgen Lawrenz. http://www.philosophos.com/philosophy_article_54.html.

23. Chiara Lubich, *Essential Writings,* 108.

24. George Steiner, *Real Presences* (Chicago: University of Chicago Press, 1991), 140.

25. Text from Ann Finch, ed., *A Star over Bethlehem: From Advent to the Epiphany* (New York and London: New City, 2001), 33.

26. Duff's comment quoted in Finola Kennedy, *Frank Duff: A Life Story* (London: Continuum, 2011), 58.

27. *True Devotion to Mary* Part 1, chapter 1, article 2.

28. Elizabeth of the Trinity, *The Complete Works. Volume One* (Washington: Discalced Carmelites, 1984), 183-84.

29. This prayer is attributed to Saint Augustine.

30. Olivier Clément, *Dialogues avec le Patriarche Athénagoras* (Paris: Fayard, 1969), 496. The text often quoted by Athenagoras orginates from Metropolitan Ignatios of Latakia (Greek Metropolitan Ignatios), speaking at the WCC, Uppsala, 1968.

NEW CITY PRESS
of the Focolare
Hyde Park, New York

About New City Press of the Focolare

New City Press is one of more than 20 publishing houses sponsored by the Focolare, a movement founded by Chiara Lubich to help bring about the realization of Jesus' prayer: "That all may be one" (John 17:21). In view of that goal, New City Press publishes books and resources that enrich the lives of people and help all to strive toward the unity of the entire human family. We are a member of the Association of Catholic Publishers.

Other Titles by Brendan Leahy

His Mass and Ours	978-1-56548-448-1	$7.95
Ecclesial Movements and Communities		
	978-1-56548-396-5	$16.95

Further Reading

Neighbors	978-1-56548-476-4	$6.95
Chiara Lubich: A Biography	978-1-56548-453-5	$14.95
Road of Hope	978-1-56548-499-3	$16.95
Gospel in Action	978-1-56548-486-3	$11.95
Tending the Mustard Seed	978-1-56548-475-7	$11.95

Periodicals
Living City Magazine,
www.livingcitymagazine.com

Scan to
join our
mailing list for
discounts and promotions
or go to
www.newcitypress.com
and click on
"join our email list."